BONZER P[...]NS™

'Cause Bonzer Means Terrific!

Published in USA, © 2022.
ISBN:978-1-66784-726-9

All I Need is a Typewriter
and a Squeaky Ball

A NOTE FROM THE AUTHOR

Given I have no thumbs, I hired Diane Wasnak as
my personal assistant. Using her mother's IBM
Selectric II, she was able to translate my observations
into this book. I hope you enjoy the poems and the
illustrations, as much as I enjoy playing
with my squeaky ball.

A bowl of water pours from the sky
    I wonder why?
I have to pee, but "Gee",
It soaks my coat, I can almost float!
My business done - it's not fun
As a two-legger wipes my paws
    And says
"Them's the Laws."

———————————————————

Cougar licks his chops,
Onto my table he hops,
As he sits on my book
He gives me a look,
And batting my pen,
It D
  R
   O
    P
    S.

Upside down led by his nose,
Bushy tail, hangs by his toes.
Grabbing all the seed to feed.
Such an acrobat indeed!
Underneath his friends below,
Wait for morsels he will throw.

I was in the ground so deep,
Through the coldness was asleep.
I could feel light so bright,
I got up with all my might.
Now the birds begin to sing,
With my trumpets come the Spring.

Outside, inside,
We're going for a ride!
Looking out the window
I barked till I cried!
The wheel turns,
My stomach churns,
Coming to a stop.
We are at the Park now,

And out I HOP !

If you see someone that's sad,
Try your best to make them glad.
There always is a way to share
A smile or touch shows you care.
Feel with an open heart
Kindness is a way to start.
There really isn't any end
Except that you have made a friend.

—————————————

While I was running all around,
Something fragrant from the ground.
It smelled so good, it made me drool,
Searching for it like a fool.
Then I found it! I dug down!
My white paws now are brown.
On my head, just a smudge
Of that fragrant oozy sludge.
Now I like the way I stink.
You should try it -
    Don't you think?

16 paws, 70 claws

8 eyes look gentle and wise.

2 ears up, 6 that sag.

4 tongues each, lick and wag.

3 short tails and one long,

Why I made this silly song.

The bright light has turned to dark
Many strange noises I hear.
I can't see, but I can bark
Bravely without fear.
A silver disk softly glows
Midst little lights that peep.
I think I'll close my eyes now
And quickly fall asleep.

Oh so softly I lick your face,
To make you well and give chase.
But for now with all my grace,
Give quiet comfort in this place.

There once was a dog who lived in a
house

That didn't have a bug, like a tick or
a louse.

As he looked out the window to watch
passersby

A buzzing he heard, and snapped at a
fly.

Waking up I shake my head
And see that I begin to shed.
I scratch my ear and scoot my rear,
Roll over on my back.
I wiggle side to side
Itching like a yak.
Up to stand, down to stare
At the rug, full of my hair.

Throw it, throw it, throw it!
But you want me to sit.
Your arm pulls back, but I must stay
Until the ball flies away.
"OK GO!", you follow through.
I know exactly what to do.
I see it as it leaves your hand
Not knowing where the ball will land.
My eyes are bugging
Legs are chugging,
I see it in the air!
Mouth wide open - LEAPING UP...
I catch it fair and square!

Much joy
Is held between my paws.
It's not a toy
That I grind with my jaws.
Much scraping
Creating and shaping.
The start
Of a new work of Art!
This sculpture of bone
Will be certainly shown
In a New York or Paris gallery.
Many will see it. I will be known
And command a very good salary!

With my paw, the bell goes "DING"!
"Get up!" I signal with the ring.
Why do people move so slow,
When the rooster starts to crow?
Pacing circles by the door,
Trying not to mess the floor.
Here they come, and just in time,
To prevent me from a crime!
Their plodding is beyond belief.
I run outside to sweet relief.

_____

I have a muse that "mews"
Who does whatever they choose.
A tail so elegant and long
Voice like a mournful song.
So silent they wander
Makes me ponder.
But why get so furious
When I am curious
To see what is in your dish?
It certainly smells like fish!
A stare with a glare
Says you won't share.
(You will scratch my nose if we fight.)
These are things I think about,
As I sit at my table and write.

Something fell from the ledge,
The human had it on the edge.
This seems to happen when they chop
Very often things will drop.
It's a mystery this treat.
I hope it's meat, or maybe sweet.
I will grab it if I'm able
Even if it's a veg-e-table!
(It's very rare that I get caught.)
I will spit it out if it's hot.

———————————————

I see you rushing all about;
You do not notice me.
I sense that you are going out,
I'm following you, see?
I watch you put your hard paws on
And tie them with a bow.
I know that you will soon be gone,
Don't leave me to my woe!
The things that jingle on a ring
You grab from off the hook.
I hope you think of me to bring,
Cannot you see my look?
But now you bolt out of the door
And leave me with the cat.
I'll never see you anymore
Or feel your gentle pat......

BUT WAIT !

You came back with my lead,

I am not left behind!

So glad you changed your mind!

_____

Pat me, pat me first now!
Can't you see I'm cute?
I can shake and I can bow,
Or bring a ball or boot.

Out of my way, I was in line;
I'll tilt my head
For scratches devine
And snuggle with you in bed.
Oh look! A hand for each of us,
There's no need to make a
fuss!

Someone's new at the door
Someone I've never seen before.
Barking, jumping, bark and jump
I nose the door with a bump.
My boss says, "SIT!" at my fit,
I do so with a thump.
As they cross the threshold
I must stay as I am told.
They hold their hand out to me;
I snuffle with much glee.
They scratch beneath my chin
And I say with a grin,
"Welcome to my home -
So glad that you came in!"

Clenching down with all my might
A sound produces when I bite.
A high pitched SQUEAK
It makes me freak!
Deep inside this toy is fluff
The task is to remove this stuff.
Both paws gripping
It starts ripping!
I have trapped it in my bed
My shark-like teeth can start to shred.
Fuzz is flying!
Victorious have I found
The mystery of this squeaky sound.

_____

Forging ahead I make safe this trail.
As your protector, I will not fail.
Back at your side I cannot see
What dangers ahead could possibly be!
A beast could pounce with teeth that gnash!
It could happen in a FLASH!
A cavernous hole where we could fall
So deep, impossible from out we crawl.
There could be muck where we get stuck,
Only way out would be a tow-truck.

So why back to your side
must you pull
When I charge forward like a bull?
I'm only trying to investigate
Dangers ahead that seal our fate.
So here by your side I'll stay in tow,
'Til the scent of most anything,
prods me to "GO"!

Fine white dust that's round
Perches above the ground
Held up by a soft green stick
Midst a blanket of yellow flowers so
thick.
Curious. As I begin to sniff
Whisps fly off as I take a whiff.
Some stick to my nose
And into the sky the rest of it goes.
There is another I try to taste.
It disappears, what a waste!
I try to catch them with a snap,
It's useless - I'll take a nap.

I found it, it's mine
It smells devine!
I think it belongs on your feet.
Did you know it tastes very sweet?
Shouting "NO!" you say
And take it away,
Turning you stomp out the door.
But what do I see on the floor?
It looks like I've seen it before.
I'll pay you no mind,
Another just like it I'll find.

———————————

In your pocket is my prize
I know I'll get if I'm wise.
When I sit,
You give a bit.
My paw to shake,
One more I'll take.
Sitting up
WOW, a cup!
Through a hoop
That's a scoop!
Over on my back I roll
I'm sure that is worth a bowl.
Look at me, around I spin!
How much is left in the bin?
Dinner time is so much fun
Getting prizes I have won!

MEET THE AUTHOR AND HIS FRIENDS

CRIKEY, the author and squeaky ball devotee, is a charming and handsome Australian Shepherd, who discovered his poetic voice during the pandemic of 2020. Born with a hearing impairment confirmed by testing at Ohio State University, it wasn't possible to measure frequency losses or any distortion, but over his first year of life some of his hearing was restored. While experiencing his other senses – the sights, the smells and the tastes of life -- Crikey began his writing journey, guided and supported by his two adopted older sisters, Bizzo & Bindi, the family cat, Cougar, and his human guardians, Diane and Barb of Bonzer Productions™.

BIZZO, a 14-year-old Australian Shepherd was mostly retired when Crikey arrived, but had performed in live shows and videos her entire life. Bizzo's career highlights include the 2010 World Equestrian Games commercial and a Telly Award for her role in Palo Alto Humane Society's 2015 educational video, "It's a Dog's Day".

BINDI, a 4 year old Australian Shepherd is building her own impressive resume, featuring her clever tricks and sweet nature in live shows, many of which are performed at retirement communities and schools.

COUGAR, a former feral feline, earned his place inside the house in the company of canines and humans, offering head rubs and his wry wit and sarcasm.

DIANE WASNAK is a physical comic, actor, and dog trainer who turned her attention to writing during the pandemic. Coming from a line of professional writers, Diane pays tribute to her mother, Lynn Wasnak, who wrote for a wide range of publications and created the newsletter, Many Voices Press, and her grandmother, Iverne Golloway-Koehler, who used various pen names and composed hundreds of children's stories for many publications between 1935 and 1975.

BARB POLK is a voiceover artist and singer, writer, videographer and editor. With live shows ceasing during the pandemic, Barb and Diane took the opportunity to write and produce videos for the Palo Alto Humane Society and their own Bonzer Productions™ YouTube channel.

MICHELLE SILVA is well known to her fans of anime and comic strip illustrations as "0becomingX". A drawing fanatic, Michelle's whimsical sketches and detailed anime characters are a lighthearted addition to Crikey's first book of poetry.

Coming Winter of 2022 from
Bonzer Productions™ . . .

"Bizzo's Holiday Secret"

A dog's story about nature,
growing up, growing old and
discovering the magic in every
season of life. This three-part
audio tale is full of fun and
enchantment.

For details, visit our website:
www.bonzerproductions.com